Putting on a Party

Adventure Parties for Kids

LORI BONNER

Illustrated by Fran Lee

Gibbs Smith, Publisher
Salt Lake City

First Edition

10 09 08 07   5 4 3 2

Text © 2004 Lori Bonner

Illustrations © 2004 Fran Lee

Published by

Gibbs Smith, Publisher

P.O. Box 667

Layton, Utah 84041

Orders (1-800) 748-5439

www.gibbs-smith.com

Designed by Fran Lee

Printed and bound in Hong Kong

Note: Some of the activities suggested in this book require adult supervision. Children and their guardians should always use common sense and good judgment in playing, cooking, and making crafts. The publisher and author assume no responsibility for any damages or injuries incurred while performing any of the activities in this book, neither are they responsible for the results of these projects.

Library of Congress Cataloging-in-Publication Data

Bonner, Lori.
Putting on a party : adventure parties for kids / Lori Bonner ;
illustrated by Fran Lee.— 1st ed.   p. cm.
Summary: Describes how to plan successful parties. Includes recipes, instructions
for making invitations and decorations, and ideas for games and activities.
ISBN 10:1-58685-232-9 ISBN 13:978-1-58685-232-0
1. Children's parties—Planning—Juvenile literature.
[1. Parties.]I. Lee, Fran, ill. II. Title.GV1205 .B62 2004
793.2'1—dc22
                                        2003019879

My reasons to celebrate:
David, Hannah, and Elijah
—LB

For my mom, Evelyn Lee,
and her mini dachshund, Lucy Lee
—FL

Contents

Let's Party!

You can have a party for many reasons. Parties are a great way to celebrate a special occasion, meet new friends, and just have fun. This book includes five great theme parties: Polar Expedition, Sensational Safari, High Seas Adventure, Space Voyage, and Westward Trek. It also includes information on everything you need to know for a successful party, from planning to party favors to being a great host. So let's get going and have fun!

Asking the Right Questions

The most important thing you can do when you are getting ready to have a party is to ask questions. These are the questions you need to answer:

- ☆ **Why?**
- ☆ **How?**
- ☆ **Where?**
- ☆ **How many?**
- ☆ **How long?**
- ☆ **Who?**
- ☆ **What?**

Once you answer these questions, you will know what you need to do to put on your party.

Why?

Ask yourself, "Why do I want to have a party?" Is it to celebrate an accomplishment such as passing a big math test, making the team, or surviving another year of piano lessons? Is it for a special event such as a birthday, holiday, or the last day of school? Is it to say good-bye to an old friend or to make a new one feel welcome? Is it just for fun? When you answer this question, you will know the reason for your party. This is important because it will help you decide who your guests will be and where and when you will have the party. It can also help you decide the theme or type of party to have and what to do at your party.

How?

Up until now, a birthday bash once a year may have been the only party you have had. Although it's fun to be surrounded by close friends who have come together with the purpose of honoring you, it is not enough experience to allow you to fully learn how to put on a party yourself. So (and this is really going to upset you), you need to have more parties.

Unless it was your mom or dad or grandma or other grown-up in charge of okaying things like parties who bought you this book, you may be thinking, "There is no way that they are going to let me have a party, especially when it's not my birthday." And the truth is, if you were to go to the person you need permission from (from now on called your "party approver," or PA) and say, "Can I have a party?" the first response very well might be "No!" Chances are, however, that they aren't being mean. They are probably remembering the last grown-up party they went to and think that they are doing you a favor. If you have ever been to a grown-up party, you know what I'm talking about: Nothing ever happens. Everyone sits around talking (ZZzzzzz). Then they eat "finger foods" (translation: vegetables). Then they talk some more (ZZzzzzz). Then everyone goes home. No one plays games or wins a prize. No one brings home something cool they made at the party. No one can say that they were on the winning team. So, it's not hard to understand why your PA might say "no" when you ask to have a party. Another reason they might say "no" is that they are really busy and they think that your having a party is going to be a lot of work and just one more thing for them to worry about.

Don't worry. The following how-to section explains a foolproof way for getting permission (almost always) to have a party.

How to Convince Your PA to Let You Have a Party:

1. Don't use the word "party." Use phrases such as "get-together," or "have a few friends over."
2. Emphasize that hosting a "social function" is good for you.
3. Tell them you think it would be good for them to know who your friends are.
4. Let them know that you will do the work and they won't have to do very much to help.
5. Promise that you'll clean up after, and then really do it.
6. Keep asking. "Fine, just stop bugging me" is almost as good as "yes."

Once you prove yourself with one party, you'll be much more likely to get a "yes" the next time you ask.

Where?

Choose a place that is safe, clean, and well supervised for your party.

"You'll catch more flies with honey than with vinegar." Have you ever heard this expression? It means you are more likely to get what you want from a nice, polite request than from a demanding, whiny one. Sincere compliments don't hurt either.

Picking out a party location first will help you know how many guests you can invite and what activities you can do at your party.

Tip: If you choose an outdoor location, have a backup indoor location in case of bad weather.

In choosing a location, also consider the purpose and theme of your party. Does it lend itself to a particular place? For example, the middle of a soccer field is a natural choice for a victory party to celebrate your team's undefeated soccer season.

Each of the parties outlined in this book contains both indoor and outdoor activities. You can mix and match activities from different parties (or use your own favorites) to create a party that's just right for your location.

How Many?

Before you put together a guest list, you have to decide how many people you can handle. This depends not only on the location of your party, but also on the age of the guests and limits set by your PA. If you have a place large enough to comfortably fit them, 10 to 12 guests is a good number for a large party. This will allow you to divide into teams, if you wish, but it is also a manageable number for group activities. If space is limited, or if you want to do more involved crafts and refreshments, then 4 to 6 guests is a good number for a smaller party.

How Long?

One factor in deciding how long your party should last is how many organized activities you want to do. If you plan on having one organized activity right after another, you will want to keep your party to about 1½ hours long. A very structured party is good if the guests don't know each other very well yet.

If you want to have quite a few organized activities but also allow for some "free time" (time to talk or play), your party should last between 2 and 2½ hours. This is also a good length for a party where only a few organized activities are planned for everyone to participate in at the same time. Such loosely structured parties are often used with very large groups.

If you want to serve a meal (rather than just refreshments), make a craft, or open or exchange gifts at your party, in addition to regular games and activities, you can plan a longer party of 2½ to 3 hours. Three hours, however, should be the longest a party should last.

A Lesson from Famous Athletes:

Famous athletes almost always retire at the end of a good season. That's because they want to go out with a "BANG!" rather than a "pppplttt" (the sound a balloon makes when you let the air out of it slowly). Instead of letting your party fizzle out, call it to an end while your guests are still having fun.

Who?

You should make a new guest list for each party that you host. This doesn't mean that all of the people on one list must be different from those on another. But it does mean that with each party, you have an opportunity to expand your social circle a little bit.

Sometimes the purpose of the party determines who is invited. For example, if you were hosting a party to celebrate the end of the year for your dance class, your guests clearly would be the members of the class, your teachers, and other people involved with your class.

If your party's purpose leaves it open as to who you invite (for example, celebrating the first snowfall or just a fun summer get-together), then here are a few suggestions that might help you to invite new people and avoid any social blunders.

 # Who to Invite?

- ☆ Someone who you play with often but who isn't necessarily a best friend.
- ☆ Someone who invited you to her party. (She probably invited you because she wanted to get to know you better or already considers you a friend.)
- ☆ Someone who you would like to get to know.
- ☆ Someone you weren't able to invite to the last party who wanted to come.
- ☆ Someone who might benefit from being included. This could be someone new in class or on the block, who could use a chance to meet people. It could be someone who has been sick and unable to play with friends for a while. It could be someone from a different religion or culture, who might otherwise feel left out in your neighborhood.
- ☆ Someone who would really, really love to be invited.
- ☆ All the members of a particular group.

Avoid the Sleeping Beauty Blunder.

Do you remember the mistake that Sleeping Beauty's parents made? They invited all the fairies of the land to her first birthday party except one. Admittedly, that one fairy wasn't the life of the party, but you don't need magic powers to know that if only one person in a group is excluded, she's going to feel bad. So, if you're thinking of inviting most of the kids on your team, in your class, or on your street, it's a good idea to invite all of them instead. Although you don't have to worry about curses if you don't, hurt and angry teammates, classmates, or neighbors can be more painful to deal with than any prick of a spinning wheel.

You should never leave people off your list to purposely make them feel bad or angry.

If you do, the purpose of your party becomes revenge. And no one has fun at a party that has the purpose of having fun without someone. Social rules for being polite, however, do not require you to invite someone who beats you to a pulp every chance he gets. In fact, if there is someone who is a physical threat to you or any of your other guests, or that your PA doesn't want you to include, leave that person off the list.

Sometimes it's just not practical or possible to include all of the people who you would like to come. Hopefully, these people can be included on your next party's guest list. Until then, use the following special how-to section to help you minimize other people's hurt feelings over not being invited this time.

Softening the Blow of Rejection

Let's get together.

What do you say when someone asks you if he can come to your party, or asks why he wasn't invited? Here's a response that works for people you wanted to include and even those you didn't. After you've explained it to them, hopefully the person will go away feeling better.

"I'm sorry, I couldn't invite everyone that I wanted to. Let's get together _____ (insert time in the near future) and _____ _____ (insert activity you could do with this person). For example, "Let's get together next Tuesday and ride bikes" or "Let's get together this weekend and watch a movie."

What?

What do you want to do at your party? Sometimes it helps to organize around a theme. A theme is just an idea you can base your party on. The five themes in this book are a polar expedition, a safari, a sea voyage, a space voyage, and a western theme. You can plan your invitations, food, decorations, games, and crafts or art projects all around the same theme.

The main things you will probably do at your party are have games and activities, crafts, and of course food. You can also have time to open presents if it is a party for a birthday or other special occasion, and time to just talk and play if you want.

Putting on the Party

Once you've made your plan and sent out the invitations, you're ready to put your plan into action. Get the decorations and the things you need for the games several days ahead. Get the things you need for the food a couple of days ahead. You will also want to decorate for your party in advance. Make sure you leave plenty of time before the party. The same with the food. Plan in advance. Some food can be made the night before; some needs to be made the day of the party. Have everything ready for when your guests arrive. You don't want to be caught decorating or only halfway through making the food when your guests arrive.

After all this planning, it's finally here! To be a good host, you will want to make sure everyone is having a good time. Welcome them when they arrive and take time to talk to each guest during the party. Follow the plan you have outlined for your activities, crafts, and food. And remember—enjoy yourself! After all, it's a party!

Tips for a Successful Party

☆ Make a plan and use it. But don't be afraid to abandon an activity that's not successful.

☆ Welcome guests as they arrive and thank them for coming. Thank them again as they leave.

☆ Have a gathering activity to involve all the guests.

☆ Talk with each guest one-on-one at least once during the party.

☆ If you have a lot of activities, do your best to make sure that each guest wins a game or is on the winning team at least once.

☆ Encourage good sportsmanship. Don't let team members be rude winners or sore losers.

My Party
* Invitations
* Decorations
* Refreshments
* Games

☆ Don't gossip to or about your guests.

☆ Practice good table manners.

☆ Allow guests to "sit out" on any activity.

☆ Relax and have fun!

After the Party

It's not over yet! You still have to clean up. Remember—you promised. If you can leave the house neater and cleaner than it was before the party, you'll probably get a "yes" the next time you want to have a party.

Polar Expedition

Invitation

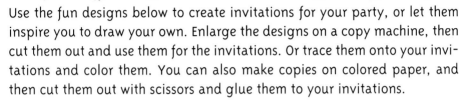

Use the fun designs below to create invitations for your party, or let them inspire you to draw your own. Enlarge the designs on a copy machine, then cut them out and use them for the invitations. Or trace them onto your invitations and color them. You can also make copies on colored paper, and then cut them out with scissors and glue them to your invitations.

Send out your written invitations two weeks before the party, if possible.
Remember to include the following information on your invitation:

★ **Purpose of the party**
★ **Date**
★ **Time**
★ **Address**
★ **Your name and phone number**
★ **Special instructions (like what to wear)**

COME AND HAVE
A (SNOW) BALL!

Given by: Jenny
Date: January 2
Time: 4p.m.-6p.m.
Address: 5 North Ave.
RSVP: 555-6787
Wear your MITTENS!

←FOLD→

You may also want to include one of the following lines for the Polar
Expedition:

★ **There's Snow Way You'll Want to Miss This!**
★ **Come and Have a (Snow) Ball!**
★ **Block Out This Day for a Party!**

Decoration Ideas

☆ Decorate a sign on a piece of poster board that says "North Pole." Hang it near the place where your guests first enter the party.

☆ Use quilt batting on furniture and tuck some around the room in nooks and crannies to look like snow.

☆ String white Christmas lights.

☆ Have friends or younger brothers and sisters help cut out snowflakes and then hang them from the ceiling with fishing line or white thread.

☆ Scatter small white balloons on the floor for snowballs.

Games and Activities
Frostbite

Warm hands and quick fingers will help your guests win this game!

Supplies needed:

- **1 wrapped candy bar**
- **Pair of mittens (not gloves)**
- **Radio or CD player**
- **Stopwatch or watch with a second hand**

How to play:

1. Seat the guests in a circle. Give the candy bar and mittens to one of the guests.
2. Start the music. The guests pass the mittens and candy bar around the circle while the music plays.
3. After 5 to 10 seconds, stop the music. Whoever has the mittens and candy bar when the music stops puts on the mittens and has 10 seconds (you'll need to time him or her) to try to open the candy bar.
4. Then start the music again and repeat. The first player able to take a bite on her turn gets to keep the candy.

Note: For more than six guests, use two pairs of mittens and two candy bars. For a large group, use three or more.

 # Iceberg Thaw

This cool activity will show you just how hot your party really is.

Supplies needed:

An ice cube for each player

How to play:

The first person to melt his ice cube wins.

There are only two rules:

1. Players may not put the ice in their mouth.

2. Only the players themselves and the clothing they are wearing may be used to melt the ice. You may want to award a cup of hot chocolate to the winner.

Penguin Race

In this relay race, your guests see how they would do as male emperor penguins, which keep their eggs warm by holding them on their feet.

Supplies needed:

1 ball of the same size for each team

How to play:

1. Set up a starting time and a turn-around point about 20 feet away. You can divide your guests into as many teams as you like, but it is better if each team has at least three players. Have the teams line up at a starting line.

2. The first member of each team places the ball between his knees. On a signal, he must "run" (it looks like a waddle) to the designated point and back without dropping the ball. Any player who drops the ball must return to the starting line and begin again.

3. Once a player makes it back to the starting line, he passes the ball to the next player. The first team to have all its players complete the run is the winning team.

 **Who won the race?**

Did you know there really is a North Pole? Both Robert E. Peary and Frederick A. Cook claim to have reached the North Pole first. Although Peary is usually given credit for reaching the pole first, on April 6, 1909, the argument has never been settled for sure.

Things to Make and Take
Snow Paint

Fresh snow becomes a giant canvas with this earth-friendly paint.

You will need:

- **Cornstarch**
- **Water**
- **Small packages of unsweetened drink mix in several different flavors (one for each spray bottle)**
- **Several small, empty spray bottles (one for each guest)**

How to make Snow Paint:

1. Place 3 tablespoons of cornstarch, 1 cup of water, and the contents of one package of drink mix in a spray bottle.

2. Shake to mix.

3. Spray the paint onto the snow to make your own masterpiece.

The Abominable Snowman

According to legend, the Abominable Snowman, also known as Yeti, is a fierce, hairy, ape-like beast that lives in Asia's mountainous arctic regions.

Tasty Treats
Apple Igloos

Makes 12 Apple Igloos

Have your guests make their own igloos.
Be sure to provide plenty of napkins.

Ingredients:

1 package (8 ounces) cream cheese, softened
1 jar (7 ounces) marshmallow creme
6 apples
I bag miniature marshmallows

Directions:

1. Beat together cream cheese and marshmallow creme in a medium bowl until smooth. You may have to stir for a while until it is smooth.

2. Wash and dry the apples. Have an adult help you cut each apple in half and carefully remove the core. Place each apple half on a plate, cut-side-down.

3. Give each guest an apple half and a butter knife. They can spread the outside of the apple with the cream cheese mixture and then press on as many marshmallows as they would like.

Snowflake Quesadillas

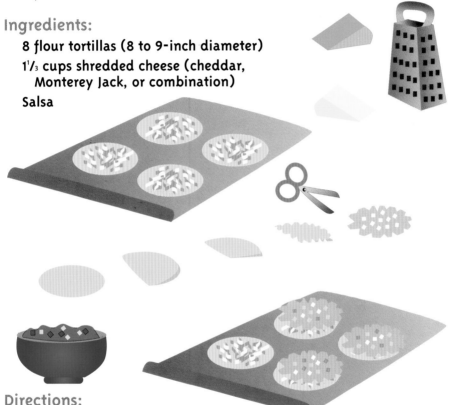

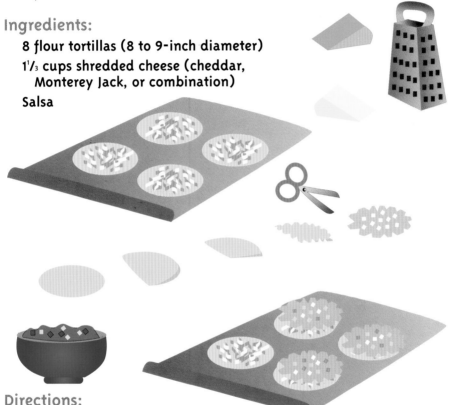

Makes 4 Snowflake Quesadillas

These yummy snacks will have your guests singing, "Let it snow, let it snow, let it snow."

Ingredients:

8 flour tortillas (8 to 9-inch diameter)

1¹⁄₃ cups shredded cheese (cheddar, Monterey Jack, or combination)

Salsa

Directions:

1. Preheat oven to 400 degrees.

2. Place 4 tortillas on a cookie sheet. Sprinkle each one with ¹⁄₃ cup cheese.

3. One at a time, place the remaining tortillas on a microwave-safe plate, cover with a paper towel, and microwave on high 10 to 15 seconds, or until soft. Gently fold each of these tortillas in half twice. Cut notches around the edges of the folded tortillas with kitchen shears or clean scissors. Unfold the cut tortillas and place them over the tortillas with cheese.

4. Bake about 5 minutes, or until cheese melts. Serve with salsa.

Sensational Safari

Invitation

Use the fun designs below to create invitations for your party, or let them inspire you to draw your own. Enlarge the designs on a copy machine, then cut them out and use them for the invitations. Or trace them onto your invitations and color them. You can also make copies on colored paper, and then cut them out with scissors and glue them to your invitations.

Send out your written invitations two weeks before the party, if possible. Remember to include the following information on your invitation:

- ⭐ **Purpose of the party**
- ⭐ **Date**
- ⭐ **Time**
- ⭐ **Address**
- ⭐ **Your name and phone number**
- ⭐ **Special instructions (like what to wear)**

Given by: Lori
Date: April 12
Time: 1p.m.-4p.m.
Address: 22 Sunny St.
RSVP: 555-2979
Wear your Safari Gear!

←FOLD→

Hunting for PARTY ANIMALS!

Given by:
Date:
Time:
Address:
RSVP:

You may also want to include one of the following lines for the Sensational Safari:

- ⭐ **Hunting for Party Animals!**
- ⭐ **It's a Party on the Wild Side!**

Decoration Ideas

⭐ Draw animal tracks with chalk on the sidewalk and driveway to lead your guests to the party entrance, or you can cut them out of construction paper and lay them out.

⭐ Fill up a wading pool with sand. Write out a sign that says "Danger: Quicksand" and place it nearby.

⭐ Bring out your stuffed animals if you have lions, tigers, snakes, elephants, or other safari-type animals, and decorate with them.

⭐ Make vines out of green and brown crepe paper to decorate the main room where the party will be.

⭐ Place potted plants, especially tall palms and ferns if you can get them, around the party area. You might be able to borrow some plants from people you know.

26

Games and Activities
Flock, Herd, or Pack

After this game, you'll be asking, "What do you call a group of party animals?"

Supplies needed:

1 large sheet of poster board
Paper and pencil for each guest

How to play:

1. Copy the directions and the two columns below onto a large sheet of poster board, or have an adult help you enlarge this list on a copy machine. Hang it in the party area.

2. As guests arrive, give them each a sheet of paper and a pencil.

3. Have the guests number their paper and match the animals to the groups.

4. Once most of the guests have arrived (about 10 minutes after the starting time of the party), give the correct answers to the game. You may wish to award a small prize to the players with the most correct answers.

Directions:

Match the name of the animal to the group it belongs in.

1. **Lion**	a. **Company**	
2. **Elephant**	b. **Flock**	
3. **Crocodile**	c. **Band**	
4. **Gorilla**	d. **Pride**	
5. **Parrot**	e. **Crash**	
6. **Viper**	f. **Herd**	
7. **Ostrich**	g. **Congregation**	
8. **Rhino**	h. **Murder**	
9. **Baboon**	i. **Nest**	
10. **Crow**	j. **Troop**	

Don't force a guest to participate in an activity. Always let them "pass" if they want to. You want everyone to be comfortable. Don't worry if they sit one out—it's no big deal.

Answers: 1(d), 2(f), 3(g), 4(c), 5(a), 6(i), 7(b), 8(e), 9(i), 10(h).

Elephant Race

This is one race your guests won't forget.

Supplies needed:

A broomstick or other long stick for each team

"Dr. Livingstone, I presume?"

Henry Morton Stanley, a newspaper reporter, was sent on assignment to Africa to find the explorer Dr. David Livingstone, since no one had heard from him in several years. (Livingstone had hoped to find a source of the Nile River south of the known source in Lake Victoria.) But instead of rushing back to report his success in finding the doctor, Stanley joined Livingstone's expedition.

Divide guests into teams by drawing an imaginary line through the middle of the room, or by having guests count off "1, 2, 1, 2," etc. Never have people pick teams. It hurts people's feelings when they are left out or chosen last.

How to play:

1. Divide into two teams.
2. Mark a starting line and turnaround point for the race. Both teams line up behind the starting line.
3. The first two members of each team stand back to back, straddling the broomstick.
4. On a signal, players race to the designated spot and back. The player facing forward on the way down should be facing backward on the way back. The first team to have each of its pairs complete the race is the winner. A small bag of peanuts is an appropriate prize.

Safari Joke

Livingstone and Stanley went out on an expedition. One night they set up their tent in a rain forest. In the middle of the night Stanley was awakened by Livingstone.

"Stanley," said Livingstone. "Do you see the lush rain forest all around us?"

"Yes," said Stanley.

"You know what that means, don't you?" asked Livingstone.

"Well," said Stanley, "it means that this rain forest, unlike many others, has not been destroyed. This is fortunate since rain forests support more than half of the world's plant and animal species, provide timber, foods, medicines, and industrial products, help to regulate the earth's climate, and maintain clean air, in addition to serving as home for millions of people."

"No, Stanley, you knucklehead!" said Livingstone. "It means that the monkeys have stolen our tent again!"

Tribal Masks

Snap a group (or rather "tribe") photo of your guests wearing these unique 3-D masks.

For each mask you will need:

Pencil

Cardboard or poster board

Scissors

Markers or crayons

Craft foam, foam sponges, or foam carpet pad (available for about $2.50 a square yard at carpet retailers)

Rubber cement

Two strips of construction paper (1 x 9 inches and 1 x 16 inches)

Tape or stapler

How to make Tribal Masks:

1. Use a pencil to draw a mask shape on the cardboard or poster board, big enough to fit over your face.

2. Trim the cardboard or poster board into the mask shape.

3. Have an adult help you cut out the eye holes.

4. Plan where you would like to have raised areas on the mask. These are the areas where you will apply shapes cut from the foam. The 3-D effect will help your mask look more like one carved from wood.

5. Color designs on the parts of the mask that will not have foam on them.

6. Cut out shapes from the foam and glue them onto the mask by applying a thin layer of rubber cement to both the foam and the cardboard or poster board where the foam will be placed.

7. Take the 16-inch strip of construction paper and glue or staple it on one side by an eyehole on the back of the mask (see illustration).

8. Glue or staple one end of the 9-inch strip of construction paper in the center of the top on the back of the mask.

9. With an adult's help, hold the mask to your face and adjust the glued strap around the back of your head until it is snug. Glue or staple it to the other side by the eyehole and trim off the extra.

10. Next, adjust the strip that comes from the top of the mask. While you hold the mask to your face, have an adult pull this strip over your head and glue, tape, or staple the strips together where they meet.

Tasty Treats
Rain Forest Refreshers

These fruit smoothies are pure paradise.

Ingredients for the fruit kabobs:

4 bamboo skewers

Assorted pieces of fruit: pineapple chunks, banana slices, grapes, straw-berries, orange slices, melon chunks, and so on (about 6 pieces per kabob)

Directions for the fruit kabobs:

1. Thoroughly wash grapes, berries, and other fresh, whole fruits. Cut up fruits as needed.

2. Carefully thread chunks of fruit onto each skewer. Place a fruit kabob in each of four 9-ounce glasses.

3. Pour in about 1 cup of the drink and serve immediately.

Be careful with the skewers. They are sharp!

Ingredients for the drink:

¾ cup (6 ounces) pineapple, orange, mango, guava, or other fruit juice or nectar

¾ cup (6 ounces) water

1 cup milk

¼ cup sugar

1 teaspoon vanilla or ½ teaspoon coconut extract

1½ cups crushed ice or 3 cups ice cubes

Directions for the drink:

1. With the help of an adult, place all ingredients in a blender.

2. Blend on high about 2 minutes, or until smooth.

3. Serve immediately with a fruit kabob in each glass.

Crocodile Hoagie

Makes 6 servings

Your guests will be relieved to be the ones doing the biting when they meet up with this crocodile!

Ingredients:

1 loaf of French bread

Butter, mayonnaise, softened cream cheese, and/or mustard

6 ounces sliced cheese

1 pound ham or combination of ham and other sliced meats

3 toothpicks

12 whole blanched almonds

2 black or green olives

Directions:

1. Cut the bread in half lengthwise so the pieces lay one on top of the other.

2. Spread the halves with butter, mayonnaise, cream cheese, and/or mustard. On the bottom half of the bread, layer cheese slices, then top with ham slices. This will be the crocodile's tongue.

3. Put the two halves of bread back together. Bend back the top half about two thirds of the way from one end, as shown. The long section will be the croc's mouth. Prop it open by placing a toothpick on the end, as shown.

4. Stick the almonds around the bottom and top edges of the mouth. These will be the teeth. (A dab of honey or cheese spread on the almonds for the top edge may help them stick.)

5. Finally, attach two black or green olives to both sides of the hoagie with the remaining toothpicks. These will be the eyes. Remove the toothpicks before serving and slice.

Invitation

Use the fun designs below to create invitations for your party, or let them inspire you to draw your own. Enlarge the designs on a copy machine, then cut them out and use them for the invitations. Or trace them onto your invitations and color them. You can also make copies on colored paper, and then cut them out with scissors and glue them to your invitations.

Send out your written invitations two weeks before the party, if possible.
Remember to include the following information on your invitation:

☆ **Purpose of the party**
☆ **Date**
☆ **Time**
☆ **Address**
☆ **Your name and phone number**
☆ **Special instructions (like what to wear)**

Given by: Johnny
Date: June 12
Time: 4p.m.-6p.m.
Address: 78 North St.
RSVP: 555-5768
Dress like a pirate!

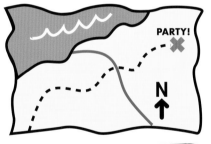

SCOPE THIS OUT:

Given by: Johnny
Date: June 12
Time: 4p.m.-6p.m.
Address: 78 North St.
RSVP: 555-5768

You may also want to include one of the following lines for the High Seas Adventure:

☆ **I Spy . . . A Party!**
☆ **Scope This Out:**
☆ **Be on the Lookout!**

 # Decoration Ideas

☆ Cut out pieces of gray construction paper in the shape of shark fins. Tape them to Popsicle sticks, dowels, or wooden skewers. Stick them in the grass near the entrance to the party.

☆ Lay a long piece of scrap lumber (approximately 1 x 4 feet) over your entranceway as a gangplank and welcome guests aboard.

☆ String up a big net and fill it with blue balloons and construction-paper fish of different colors.

☆ If your party is inside, cover the windows in the main party area halfway up with blue cellophane or construction paper so that it looks like you are below deck on a boat.

☆ Place rope coils, life jackets, a world map or globe, and/or a blow-up raft in a central area.

"Walking the Plank"

Pirates would sometimes force prisoners to "walk the plank" off the ship into the ocean, where they would meet a watery end.

Games and Activities
Lifeboat

Your guests will enjoy this hilarious twist on musical chairs.

Supplies needed:

1 less chair than the number of guests you have

How to play:

1. Place chairs in a circle.

2. Have the guests walk around the circle of chairs until you yell, "To the lifeboats!" All the guests race for a chair. The guest without a chair simply sits on a chair with someone else.

3. Remove a chair and have the guests walk around the circle again. Then yell, "To the lifeboats!" Repeat this until all the guests are on one chair!

For warm-weather fun, set up the chairs on the grass and place sprinklers under one or more of them.

Treasure Hunts

Few things are more fun for a High Seas Adventure party than a treasure hunt. Each of these treasure hunts has to be set up before the party begins.

Buried Treasure

1. For an outdoor activity, bury wrapped candies, coins, and toys in a sandbox and allow the guests to dig for them. Provide guests with buckets and small shovels or spoons.

2. If you don't have a sandbox available, or if you want to do an indoor activity, place some pine bedding (used for guinea pigs and other small animals) in the bottom of a large container (a plastic storage tote is ideal).

3. Hide candy, coins, and small trinkets in the bedding, or hide pennies or plastic coins that guests can redeem for candy and other items at a "treasure store" that you set up.

4. Allow each guest (or group of two or three guests, depending on the size of the container you're using) 10 seconds to find what they can.

5. After all guests have had a chance to search once, you can give everyone a second try. On the second time around, however, start with the people who went last the first time.

Treasure Hunt with Object Clues

1. Gather objects that fit the High Seas Adventure theme, such as a seashell, a net, a sailor's hat, a model ship, and so on.

2. Place a piece of paper inside each object with either a picture or the name of the next object they are to find written on it.

3. Hide the objects in your yard.

4. When you are ready to play, give guests the first clue. The last clue should lead them to the treasure.

Treasure Map

1. Make a map that shows the treasure's location.

2. Cut it into several pieces.

3. Give the group a piece after they complete each organized activity at the party, such as the "Lifeboat" game, the "Parroting Parrots" game, or making a pirate hat.

4. After they have collected all the pieces by the end of the party, have them put together the map as a group and follow it to the treasure.

Guess the Number Treasure Hunt

1. Provide each guest with a piece of paper and a pencil.

2. In this hunt, you hide various items that hold many smaller parts, such as a jar of small candies. The guests will find the items and then guess how many of the smaller things each item holds. The guest who comes closest to the actual number for each item gets to take that item home.

A few suggestions to use for treasure:

☆ a jar filled with small candies (M&Ms, Skittles, etc.)

☆ a plate of chocolate chip cookies (how many chocolate chips— be sure to count the chocolate chips before you make the cookies)

☆ a small cloth sack filled with pennies or marbles (they can feel the bag to make their guess)

☆ a bag of popcorn (how many kernels?)

☆ a watermelon (how many pounds?)

☆ a rope of licorice (how many inches?)

Note: You will have to figure out the correct answer for each item before the party. Also, in order to avoid confusion, each item should have a label or sign of some type that says what thing the guests are supposed to estimate. It is also helpful to give each item a name or number and have the guests write this name or number next to their guess for that item.

Are you in the Doldrums?

Your High Seas Adventure should keep you and your guests out of the doldrums. The Doldrums is a region near the equator where ships become sluggish because the air moves upward instead of crosswise. People use the word "doldrums" to mean that something is boring.

Parroting Parrots

Large groups work best for this activity.

How to play:

1. Have your guests sit in a circle.

2. Whisper a message into the ear of the guest on your right. This guest in turn must repeat, or "parrot," the message to the guest on her right. Each person may say it only once.

3. Continue in this way until you get to the last guest in the circle.

4. The last person should stand up and repeat the message out loud. It is fun to compare it with the original message.

Tongue twisters make this game even more fun. Here are three High Seas Adventure messages you can use. Or you can write your own.

1. Smiling sailors share several secret ships.

2. Plundering pirates pluck and pilfer plentiful pansies.

3. Five fresh flying fish flew freely.

Thmiling snailors stare shevral shekret chips . . .

Keep whispering confined to the Parroting Parrots game. Never say anything negative to one of your guests about another guest or about someone who is not at the party.

Things to Make and Take
Scrimshaw

During long voyages, many sailors carved images on whalebones or shells. These engravings are called scrimshaw.

For each guest you will need:
1 bar of smooth white soap
1 sharpened pencil
1 butter knife
Watercolors (optional)

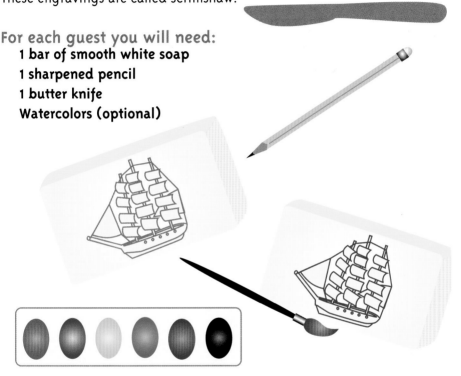

How to make your own Scrimshaw:

1. Set up this activity outside or in an area that can be easily swept. Provide each guest with a bar of soap to carve. Each guest will use a sharpened pencil as a carving tool.

2. Scratch your design or picture into the soap first. It can be erased by gently scraping with a butter knife. Once you are satisfied with the carving, go over the lines again and again to deepen them. You will need to blow the soap shavings from the lines as you go. Be careful not to blow them onto other guests. For a sharper image, brush over your carving with a thin layer of watercolors.

Tasty Treats
Limey-Aid

Makes 8 servings

A secret ingredient turns ordinary lemon-lime soda into a refreshing drink named after early British sailors, or "limeys."

Ingredients:

1 large lime

Ice

1 bottle (at least 24 ounces) white grape juice (do not use regular purple grape juice)

1 (2-liter) bottle lemon-lime soda

Straws

Directions:

1. Wash the lime in warm, soapy water. Rinse well and pat dry with a paper towel. Slice the lime into eight wedges.

2. Fill 8 (16-ounce) glasses with ice. Use the ounce measurement on a liquid measuring cup to help you pour 3 ounces of white grape juice into each glass. Squeeze the juice from a lime wedge into each glass and then drop in the lime slice. Fill each glass to within ½ to 1 inch of the top with soda. Stir each drink gently with a straw before serving.

You can also make Limey-Aid in a punch bowl. Just keep the ratio of 1 cup of white grape juice to 3 cups of soda (1:3) about the same. To make 1 gallon, add 1 quart of juice to 3 quarts of soda. Use 2 limes per gallon of beverage.

Did you know?

British sailors were sometimes called "limeys" because they would eat limes on their voyages to prevent scurvy, a disease caused by a lack of vitamin C. Limes and other citrus fruits, such as oranges and lemons, are a good source of vitamin C.

Walk the Plank Fries
(with Shiver Me Timbers Sauce)

Makes 4 to 6 servings

Although these tasty taters are delicious served with burgers, hot dogs, or Turtle on a Stick, they are so hearty that they make a great lunch all by themselves.

Ingredients:

- 6 medium russet potatoes
- 2 tablespoons taco seasoning mix
- 2 tablespoons vegetable oil
- ¼ cup ketchup
- 2 tablespoons bottled barbecue sauce
- 1 cup mayonnaise
- 1 cup shredded cheese (optional)

Directions:

1. Preheat oven to 325 degrees.

2. Using a vegetable brush, scrub potatoes under warm water. Have an adult help cut off any bruises or eyes. Cut each potato in 4 parts lengthwise.

3. Place the potato planks in a large bowl. Sprinkle the taco seasoning mix on top, then drizzle the oil over them. Toss the potatoes until they are evenly coated.

4. Spray a baking sheet with nonstick spray. Arrange potatoes, with a cut side down, in a single layer on the baking sheet. Bake for 1 hour.

5. Prepare sauce while potatoes are baking. In a medium bowl, stir ketchup and barbecue sauce into mayonnaise until thoroughly blended. Store the sauce in the refrigerator until serving time.

6. Remove potatoes from oven after one hour and increase oven temperature to 425 degrees. Using tongs, have an adult help you turn each plank. Place potatoes back in the oven 15 minutes longer until brown and crispy. Turn oven off. Sprinkle potatoes with cheese, if using. Allow to stand in hot oven 3 to 5 minutes, or until cheese is melted.

7. Using a pancake turner, transfer potatoes to a serving platter. Serve with the sauce on the side.

Space Voyage

Invitation

Use the fun designs below to create invitations for your party, or let them inspire you to draw your own. Enlarge the designs on a copy machine, then cut them out and use them for the invitations. Or trace them onto your invitations and color them. You can also make copies on colored paper, and then cut them out with scissors and glue them to your invitations.

Send out your written invitations two weeks before the party, if possible. Remember to include the following information on your invitation:

- ☆ **Purpose of the party**
- ☆ **Date**
- ☆ **Time**
- ☆ **Address**
- ☆ **Your name and phone number**
- ☆ **Special instructions (like what to wear)**

COME FOR A PARTY

THAT'S OUT OF THIS WORLD!

Given by: Sarah
Date: April 12
Time: 4p.m.- 6p.m.
Address: 22 Sunny St.
RSVP: 555-2979

Outside →

Inside ↓

You may also want to include one of the following lines for the Space Voyage:

- ☆ **Prepare to Have a Blast!**
- ☆ **It's a UFO! (Unbelievably Fun Occasion)**
- ☆ **Come for a Party That's Out of This World!**

It's a UFO!
(**U**nbelievably
Fun **O**ccasion)
Given by: Sarah
Date: April 12
Time: 4p.m.-6p.m.
Address: 22 Sunny St.
RSVP: 555-2979

⭐ ⭐ ⭐ Decoration Ideas ⭐ ⭐ ⭐

⭐ Make a mileage sign out of poster board and stick it near the entrance to the party.

    Jupiter 600,000,000 miles

    Mars   34,600,000 miles

    Sun   93,000,000 miles

    Party   10 feet!

⭐ Cover the table with foil or black butcher paper decorated with star stickers or confetti. You can cut stars out of aluminum foil and tape them to the butcher paper.

⭐ Draw big, oval-shaped eyes with a black marker on lime-green helium balloons to make "aliens."

⭐ Cover windows with black butcher paper covered with star stickers.

⭐ Pick streamers and other paper products in black, dark blue, or silver.

⭐ String up white or clear lights.

Games and Activities
Comet Tag

Play this game outside.

How to play:

Have the guests form a line with each person holding onto the waist of the person in front of him. The person at the front of the line is the Head and the person at the back is the Tail. The Head tries to tag the Tail. If she is successful, she moves back one space in line and the Tail goes to the front of the line and becomes the new Head. If the line breaks before the Head catches the Tail, the person at the back of the break must take the place of the Head, who, in turn, moves back one space in line. Play until everyone has had a chance to be either the Head or the Tail.

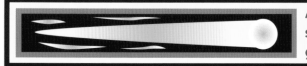

A comet is a big, dirty snowball with a tail of gas and dust.

The Astrologer

An astrologer is someone who claims to know and interpret the supposed influence of the stars and planets on people and events.

Supplies needed:

> **1 empty can with a plastic lid, such as a coffee can or snack chip canister**
>
> **Construction paper to decorate the can and to make square answer card**
>
> **Scissors**
>
> **Glue**

I can predict the future. . . !

Make this before your party:

1. Decorate the outside of the can with construction paper and star stickers.

2. Cut out two identical squares of construction paper small enough to move around when the can is shaken and to lie flat on the bottom of the can.

3. Glue the squares together and let dry.

4. After the glue is dry, write "Most Likely" on one side, and "Probably Not" on the other.

5. Place the square in the can and put on the lid.

How to play:

1. Have the guests sit in a circle. Explain that the can you hold is called "The Astrologer" because it is sensitive to the movements of the cosmos (the universe) and can predict the future.

2. Choose one of your guests and have her ask a question about her future that could be answered "yes" or "no." Shake the can and then open the lid to reveal the answer.

3. Then pass the can to the person who asked the question. Now it is her turn to pick someone else in the circle to ask "The Astrologer" a question. Keep playing until everyone has had a turn.

Things to Make and Take
Alien Slime

This wonderful goo is made by mixing equal parts of liquid starch and white school glue—a perfect project for your guests to make.

You will need:

- ¹/₄ cup liquid starch
- Disposable plastic container (like a whipped topping container)
- Food coloring
- 1 bottle (7 ounces) white school glue
- Plastic spoon
- Zipper-seal sandwich bags or plastic eggs

How to make Alien Slime:

1. Place the liquid starch into the plastic container. Stir in 7 to 8 drops of food coloring; use more or less, depending on the shade you want.
2. Slowly pour the glue into the starch, stirring constantly with the plastic spoon. The glue will thicken and become ropey.
3. Knead the mixture with your hands (let your guests take turns) until all of the liquid starch is absorbed. Let the mixture stand for five minutes.
4. Turn the alien slime onto a smooth countertop or tabletop and knead again until it is smooth.
5. Break off a blob for everyone. Play with it.
6. Give each guest a zipper-seal sandwich bag or a plastic egg to store his slime in.

Have slime races:

Everyone positions their slime on the edge of a table or countertop. On a signal, everyone pushes part of their slime over the edge to start it stringing out toward the floor. The first player whose slime string reaches the floor is the winner.

Warning: Place the slime only on smooth countertops, tabletops, or floors. It will stick to paper, fabric, and carpet.

Moon Rocks

These make a great souvenir for your guests to take home from the Space Voyage. To surprise your guests when they crack open their rocks, either make the rocks yourself in advance, or give each guest a different rock to take home than the one he made at the party.

You will need:

Disposable plastic bowl

1 cup clean play sand (sold in bags at home improvement and hardware stores)

½ cup flour

Silver glitter

¼ cup water, or more if needed

Tiny plastic toys or coins

Small hammer

How to make Moon Rocks:

1. In a disposable plastic bowl (whipped topping containers work well), stir together the sand, flour, and enough glitter to make the mixture sparkle.

2. Stir in ¼ cup water. Mix until all of the sand is moistened and the mixture forms a very stiff dough. Add additional water, one teaspoon at a time, if needed.

3. Take a clump of the sand dough, about the size of a golf ball. Flatten it in the palm of your hand. Place a toy or coin in the center of the dough. Carefully mold the dough around the toy to cover it completely.

4. Cover a cookie sheet with foil. Spray the foil with nonstick coating. Place the moon rocks on the cookie sheet. Allow them to dry and harden in a sunny spot for at least two days.

5. After the moon rocks are completely dry, instruct your guests to tap them with a hammer to split them open and reveal the treasure inside.

Tasty Treats
Flying Saucer Meat Pies

Makes 5 servings, 2 saucers each

These tasty meat pies are out of this world!

Ingredients:

Foil
1 package (8 ounces) cream cheese, softened
2 cups diced cooked chicken
1 green onion, finely chopped
2 cans (7 ounces each) refrigerated buttermilk biscuits
½ cup (1 stick) butter or margarine, melted
1 box (6 ounces) seasoned croutons, crushed

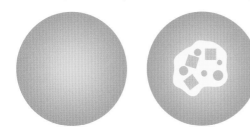

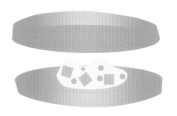

Directions:

1. Preheat the oven to 350 degrees. Line the bottom of a cookie sheet or jellyroll pan with foil.

2. In a small bowl, stir together the cream cheese and chicken and green onion.

3. On a lightly floured smooth surface, roll each biscuit into a 3 ½-inch circle.

4. Place 2 heaping tablespoons of the chicken and cream cheese mixture onto the center of 5 of the circles.

5. Place the other 5 circles over the filled circles and pinch around the edges of each "flying saucer" to seal.

6. Dip each saucer in the melted butter and then in the crouton crumbs, coating both sides. Place the saucers on the prepared cookie sheet.

7. Bake 15 to 20 minutes, or until golden brown.

Plutonian Freeze

Transform frozen fruit and yogurt into a delicious concoction at light speed with this easy recipe.

Ingredients:

3 cups bite-size unsweetened fruit pieces, frozen
1 container (8 ounces) yogurt, any flavor
1 cup powdered sugar

Directions:

1. For the fruit, you can use packaged unsweetened fruit such as peaches, berries, or mixed fruit. You can also prepare your own. To do so, place pieces of fruit in a single layer on a cookie sheet sprayed with nonstick coating. Strawberries cut in half, banana slices, and chunks of mango, melon, and pineapple are a few suggestions. Freeze for 2 to 3 hours, or until firm.

   To prevent the bananas from turning brown, toss them with some lemon juice before freezing.

2. Have an adult prepare the knife-blade attachment for the food processor. Place the frozen fruit in the processor's container. Process the fruit, stopping to scrape down the sides occasionally, until it is very finely chopped.

3. Add the yogurt. Choose a flavor that complements your choice of fruit. For example, lemon is good with berries, peach is good with peaches, and so on. Then add the powdered sugar. Process this mixture, again stopping to scrape down the sides occasionally, until smooth. You can serve this immediately, or transfer it to a freezer container and freeze for an hour or more, then scoop it out with an ice-cream scoop.

Now That's Cold!

Pluto is about 39 times farther from the sun than Earth is. Pluto's temperature is more than 350 degrees below zero. It is one of the coldest places in our solar system.

Invitation

Use the fun designs below to create invitations for your party, or let them inspire you to draw your own. Enlarge the designs on a copy machine, then cut them out and use them for the invitations. Or trace them onto your invitations and color them. You can also make copies on colored paper, and then cut them out with scissors and glue them to your invitations.

Send out your written invitations two weeks before the party, if possible. Remember to include the following information on your invitation:

- ★ **Purpose of the party**
- ★ **Date**
- ★ **Time**
- ★ **Address**
- ★ **Your name and phone number**
- ★ **Special instructions (like what to wear)**

Given by: Alice

Date: August 30

Time: 2p.m.-5p.m.

Address: 16 Hart St.

RSVP: 555-9721

Wear your cowboy duds

You may also want to include one of the following lines for the Westward Trek:

- ★ **Circle Your Wagons!**
- ★ **Trek on Over!**
- ★ **Round Up for a Good Time!**

☆ Place a bale of hay near the entrance. Write out a sign to put with it that says, "Hay! The Party's Here!"

☆ Transform a part of the party's location into a makeshift campsite. Place some red Christmas lights or a flashlight underneath a pile of sticks. For flames, crumple red and yellow cellophane and stuff it into the pile. You can also make a circle of rocks around the pile. Use blankets or quilts placed around the fire for guests to sit on. If the party is outdoors, you could also use bales of hay for seating.

☆ Decorate with "supplies," such as a lantern, rope coils, and white pillowcases stuffed with newspaper and labeled "Flour Sacks."

☆ Use pie tins for plates and pint jars for cups.

☆ As each guest arrives, give her a bandana to tie on her head or around her neck. Use several different colors of bandanas and have all the guests with one color form a team. Let guests take theirs home as a party favor.

Games and Activities
Fox and Geese

Your guests will enjoy this tag game as much as frontier children did.

To prepare for the game:

1. Draw a huge wagon wheel on the ground for this game. Start by making a large circle (about 25 feet across).
2. You can draw the circle in the dirt, use chalk on cement or pavement, or use Snow Paint in the snow. You may want an adult to help you with this. (See page 21 for instructions on how to make Snow Paint.)
3. Next, draw eight spokes inside the circle by drawing four lines that intersect in the center, as when slicing a pie (see illustration).

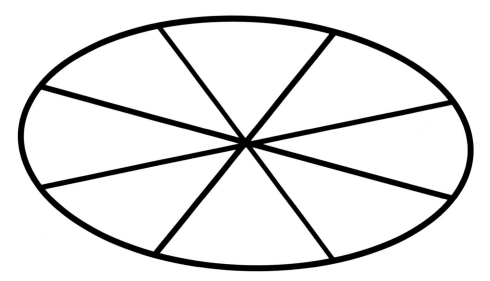

How to play:

1. Choose one player to be the Fox. He chases the other players (the Geese) up and down the spokes and around the circle. The Geese have to stay on the line of the wagon wheel. There is no home base.
2. When a Goose is tagged, she becomes the Fox.

Johnny Appleseed Race

Your guests will need teamwork to suc-"seed" in this race.

Supplies needed:

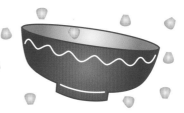

1 bowl for each team
25 corn kernels in each bowl

How to play:

1. Divide into teams of at least four players each. Have the teams line up single file. In front of each team, put a bowl of about 25 corn kernels. At the end of each team's line, place an empty bowl. The object of the game is to get the most kernels from the bowl in the front of the line to the bowl at the end of the line.

2. On a signal, the first player in each team picks up one kernel from the bowl and passes it to the player behind him without looking back.

3. The second player takes the kernel and passes it on. When the kernel reaches the end of the line, the last player reaches back and puts it into the empty bowl. No peeking!

4. As soon as she drops it in the bowl, she yells, "More seeds, Johnny," and the first player starts another kernel down the line. After about 5 minutes, call stop. The team with the most kernels in the bowl at the end of their line wins.

5. For warm-weather fun, replace the bowls with buckets, one of which is full of water. Give each player a cup. Have the first player dip her cup into the bucket of water. That person then pours it over her shoulder. The player behind tries to catch the water in his cup. The water continues down the line in this way until the last person in line pours it over his shoulder into the empty bucket. After time is called, the team with the most water in the bucket at the end of the line wins.

"Johnny Appleseed" was the nickname of American pioneer John Chapman. He became famous for planting apple trees along the frontier.

Things to Make and Take
Tin Lantern

Because tin is lightweight, durable, and easily shaped, it was often used by pioneers for plates, cups, candlesticks, boxes, and lanterns. To prevent rusting, tinsmiths coated the tin with a tar-based shellac that turned the metal black. Colorful designs were then painted on the tin, or designs were made by punching holes in a decorative pattern.

For each lantern you will need:

A tall, clean, empty tin can, with any labels removed
1 (24-inch piece) heavy string or cord
1 long nail with a wide, flat head, such as a sinker nail
A strip of paper cut to fit around the can
Pencil
Masking tape
Hammer
Ruler
1 votive candle

How to make the lantern:

1. The day before the party, fill the cans ¾ full of water and freeze. This will keep the sides of the can from crushing in as you punch your design into the lantern.

2. Cover the work surface with cardboard or a tablecloth to protect against scratches.

3. Pick a design from those illustrated above, or draw your own simple design on paper. Tracing a cookie cutter is an easy way to make a design too.

4. With a pencil, you will need to mark where the holes will be punched— about every half inch.

5. You will also need to mark two holes, across from each other, about one inch from the top of the can. You will use these holes for your lantern's handle.

6. Tape the paper to the outside of the can.

7. Gently hammer a nail through the can where you have marked it on your design. If your designs are small or the marks very close together, just tap the hammer until the tip of the nail makes a tiny hole, rather than allowing the entire end of the nail to go through the can.

8. After all the holes are punched, remove the paper.

9. Thread one end of the string or cord through the handle holes. Tie the ends of the cord together. You can use this to carry your lantern, since a lighted candle will cause the can to become hot to the touch.

10. Choose a candle that is several inches shorter than the height of the can. Place the candle in the lantern. Have an adult light the candle with a long match. Make sure that you always keep the handle away from the lantern's flame. Never leave a burning candle unattended!

Tasty Treats
Oregon Trail Pizza

Makes 4 to 6 servings

The surface of this tasty pizza is bumpy and uneven, a lot like the 2,000-mile Oregon Trail that hundreds of thousands of settlers followed across the Great Plains and Rocky Mountains into Oregon.

Ingredients:

- 2 cans (7 ounces each) refrigerated buttermilk biscuits
- 1 can or jar (8 to 16 ounces) tomato, pizza, or spaghetti sauce
- Choice of toppings: pepperoni,* ham slices,* mushrooms, pineapple chunks, black olives, diced green pepper
- 2 cups shredded cheese (mozzarella and cheddar are a good combination)

*Use only precooked meats.

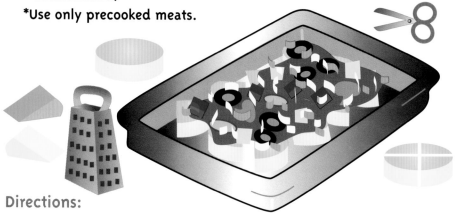

Directions:

1. Preheat oven to 400 degrees.

2. Spray a 9 x 13-inch baking pan with nonstick coating. Using a pair of clean scissors, cut each biscuit into quarters. Scatter biscuit pieces over the bottom of the baking pan. Spoon sauce over the biscuit pieces. Use more sauce if you like your pizza really "saucy" and less if you don't. Sprinkle with your choice of toppings and finish off with the cheese. Bake for 18 to 25 minutes, or until the biscuits are golden brown.

Safety Tip: Always have an adult supervise when you are using the oven or stove.

Prairie Pies

These big chocolate cookies look like gooey cow pies. But they smell a lot better!

Ingredients:

1 box chocolate cake mix
½ cup vegetable oil
2 eggs
2 cups chocolate chips

Directions:

1. Preheat oven to 350 degrees.
2. Combine cake mix, oil, and eggs in a large bowl. Stir in chocolate chips.
3. Use ¼ cup of dough for each Prairie Pie, placing them about 3 inches apart onto ungreased cookie sheets. Flatten each cookie a little bit with the bottom of a measuring cup. Bake 12 to 15 minutes, or until centers are just set. Let cookies stand two minutes; remove to racks or counter-top to cool. Store in an airtight container to retain softness.

When there was no wood to burn while they were crossing the plains, pioneers often made their campfires out of dried cow pies.

Purple Cows

Enjoy these divine "bovine" floats!

Ingredients:

Vanilla ice cream
Grape soda

Directions:

Put a scoop of vanilla ice cream in a glass, then fill it up with grape soda. Use root beer or cola for Brown Cows.

Planning the Next Party!

The party is over. But your job isn't. You need to evaluate. This means you need to figure out which parts of your party were a success and what things you could improve on next time. Do it now, while the party is still fresh in your mind. Use the paper you made the party's plan on to help you.

First, which things were a hit? Make a note next to the favorite games and activities. Also note ones that were not as fun. Next, think about the order of the activities. Did it work well? Would you change anything around next time? Finally, think about the party as a whole. Was the party's purpose carried out? Did everyone seem to have a good time? How did this party compare to other parties? Be sure to write down anything that you would like to try differently in the future. Now put the paper in a safe place (along with this book) so that you will be able to find them when you plan your next party.

P.S. Don't forget to clean up!

My Party
*Invitations
*Decorations
*Refreshments
*Games

Collect them all!

Available at bookstores or directly from
GIBBS SMITH, PUBLISHER
1.800.748.5439/www.gibbs-smith.com